THE MARTYR OF EL SALVADOR

THE ASSASSINATION OF ÓSCAR ROMERO

COLD CASE CRIME SERIES #2

REAGAN MARTIN

Absolute Crime Press
ANAHEIM, CALIFORNIA

ABSO UTE
CR ME

www.AbsoluteCrime.com

Contents

ABOUT ABSOLUTE CRIME

Absolute Crime publishes only the best true crime literature. Our focus is on the crimes that you've probably never heard of, but you are fascinated to read more about. With each engaging and gripping story, we try to let readers relive moments in history that some people have tried to forget.

Remember, our books are not meant for the faint at heart. We don't hold back--if a crime is bloody, we let the words splatter across the page so you can experience the crime in the most horrifying way!

If you enjoy this book, please visit our homepage (www.AbsoluteCrime.com) to see other books we offer; if you have any feedback, we'd love to hear from you!

Sign up for our mailing list, and we'll send you out a free true crime book! http://www.absolutecrime.com/newsletter

PROLOGUE

March 12, 1977 was a Saturday, and Father Rutilio Grande was running late. He was scheduled to say the evening mass at El Paisnal, a small rural community near San Salvador, and Manuel Solórzano and Nelson Lemus, two men who had come to drive him to the church, were already waiting for him.

Manuel was 72-years-old, kind, gentle, and exceedingly loyal to Father Grande. Nelson, on the other hand, was still a boy at 15, but the environment he had been born and raised in had stolen his youth and forced him to become a man far too soon. Not his home environment, for his family was extremely close and god-fearing, but the environment his government had created for its subjects.

The country of El Salvador was ruled by a brutal and sadistic regime that cared nothing about the exceedingly poor people who lived there, or the hardships they endured on a daily basis. They viewed the peasants, those like Manuel and Nelson, and all the other people Father Grande ministered to, as 'sub-humans' with little value, and even less worth.

As Father Grande adjusted the white Roman collar on his clerical suit, he thought about the climate of fear that was escalating in his country, and he was deeply concerned by it. There was a time when priests were looked upon as holy and respectable men in El Salvador, but not any longer. At least not to the hierarchy of the country.

Faith and preaching were actions that were contrary to the government's beliefs, and the Bible was not viewed as the word of God, but as a subversive book designed to overthrow their rule. Priests all over the country were coming under attack by ruthless military soldiers. They were being harassed and abused, and often deported for little more than preaching the gospel.

Only a month earlier, a Columbian priest had been exiled from the country for holding mass, an act that inspired Father Grande to give a sermon that drew sharp criticism from the Salvadoran government.

Telling his congregation that he feared the Holy Bible would soon be banned from their country, Father Grande continued his sermon in a sarcastic manner;

"The Bible is subversive – after all, all of its pages are against sin. If Jesus of Nazareth returned today, I dare say he would not arrive with preaching and actions. They, [the Salvadoran government], would arrest him for being a subversive and crucify him again!"

The sermon had rallied the peasant congregation, but Father Grande knew it had infuriated the regime and its military. He was concerned, not for his own safety, for he had no fear of death, but for the peasants he ministered too, and what would become of them if something were to happen to him.

He would like to think the church would continue his work, but he was not convinced that they would. Only a month earlier, in February, Archbishop Luis Chavez, a humanitarian who shared Father Grande's concern for the peasant population, had reached the mandatory age of retirement, and was replaced by Archbishop Oscar Romero. Although Rutilio Grande and Oscar Romero were close friends, Grande was disappointed by the replacement.

Oscar Romero was known to be a staunch conservative who kept the church and political climate totally separate, a fact, Father Grande was certain, which had a lot to do with his appointment as Archbishop. The church, as well as the government and military of El Salvador wanted someone like Romero to head the church. Someone who would preach non-violence and quell the rising anger in the unhappy peasants. With Romero now in control, Father Grande feared that any progress made with the downtrodden of the country would be completely reversed.

But Father Grande couldn't think about that right now. He was already late and Manuel Solórzano was calling to him for the second time.

"I'm coming." The priest called back to his waiting helpers. Hastily grabbing his hat, Father Grande went outside and climbed into the passenger seat of the waiting car.

Manuel was driving, and Nelson sat in the backseat as the vehicle pulled away and began traveling down the dirt road. Their destination was rural, and they drove between fields brimming with sugar cane. Father Grande's mind was wandering once again, and he made a mental note to contact his old friend, the new Archbishop Romero, to discuss the work with the peasants he felt needed to continue.

But Father Grande would never get the chance. Out of nowhere, a spray of machine gun fire erupted, rat-a-tat-tatting at a nonstop pace, pelting the car with bullets that ripped through the metal like tissue paper, and piercing its targets inside. No one in the car had time to react. All three were hit almost simultaneously, and the car, no longer under control, veered off the road and plowed through a hedge of sugar cane.

Manuel Solórzano, Nelson Lemus, and Father Rutilio Grande were dead, and although he didn't know it at the time, the murders were a warning to Father Grande's good friend, the new Archbishop, Oscar Romero.

CHAPTER 1

Oscar Romero was born on August 15, 1917, the second of seven children to Guadalupe and Santos Romero, in Ciudad Barrios, a small Salvadoran mountain town. By American standards even back then, the Romeros would have been considered dirt poor, although in their small village they had more than most.

They lived in a tiny adobe hut with no electricity or running water and so little room that the children were forced to sleep on the floor. But the Romeros were a happy and loving family, very religious, and dedicated to their Roman Catholic faith. Each of the children would attend school until the age of twelve, and then be apprenticed out to find work and help support the family.

From the time he was little, Oscar had developed a deep love for his Church, and a strong faith in God. He always knew he wanted to become a priest, but at the age of 12 his parents apprenticed him out to a carpenter, where it was discovered that he was extremely skilled in this occupation. He could have gone on to have a successful career in it, but his calling to the priesthood had never diminished, and at the age of 13 he entered the minor seminary in San Miguel.

From there, he would continue his service at the national seminary in San Salvador and eventually move on to the Gregorian University in Rome. His studies now complete, he received a Licentiate in Theology and was ordained in 1942 at the age of 25.

WWII was at its peak at the time, and the young priest was kept busy in Italy, far from his home. The war had restricted travel between countries, and it would be several years before Oscar saw his family again.

In 1944, when El Salvador experienced a shortage of priests, Oscar was called back home and given a small rural parish to serve over. Father Romero had a knack for oration, and word quickly spread of his powerful and meaningful sermons. People came from all over to hear the pastor preach, and he soon became extremely popular with his congregants.

His superiors in the diocese also noted that Romero had a God-given gift, and before long they had appointed him rector of the inter-diocesan seminary, and secretary of the Diocese of San Miguel. Romero was pleased. It was an impressive achievement for the poor boy who had grown up in the mountains of El Salvador.

Oscar was aware of what was happening to the less fortunate around him, and although sympathetic to their plight, he felt it was none of his business, just like it was none of the church's business. Oscar Romero was a firm believer in the separation of church and state, and his belief was that the church should not meddle in what the government was doing, no matter how bad it might be.

For years, El Salvador had been ruled by a military dictatorship, controlled by an oligarchy, or small governing body, comprised of the wealthiest families in the nation. This aristocracy, commonly referred to as the '14 families', had made their riches off of huge coffee plantations, using their own people as slave labor.

For decades, the class distinction between El Salvador's hierarchy and the country's peasants, or campesinos, was transparently obvious. Of the country's 5 million people more than half, or approximately 3.5 million of them, lived on less than $1.00 a day. At the same time, some families in the country were making more than $10,000 dollars a month, and the wealthiest made far more than that.

While the rich of El Salvador lived lavish lifestyles, the peasants struggled to survive in abject poverty. But complaints from the campesinos were not tolerated, and instantly met with brutal reprisal from the Salvadoran military. Any action contrary to the views of the hierarchy were deemed to be communist, Marxist, or subversive. This included the Catholic Church and those who worked or worshiped in it. The Catholic Church, the Salvadoran government claimed, favored the spread of Marxism.

Of course, there were times when the campesinos did rebel against their oppressive treatment, even uprising against their government. But their reward for this effort whenever they did was a slaughtering of their people on a massive scale. The peasants found it difficult to fight against a military that had major allies backing it.

One of El Salvador's strongest supporters was the United States. Beginning back in the Kennedy administration, America's troubles with Cuba and the Soviet Union had propelled the U.S. to begin a war on communism that would come to be known as the Cold War. Any countries dealing with communist insurgents could appeal to the U.S. for help and support, knowing they would receive it.

While many of the campesinos in El Salvador might have been pro-communist, that didn't necessarily mean they were pro-Soviet Union or pro-Cuba. What the peasants of the country wanted was simply what most people take for granted every day; fair working conditions, better and equal wages, access to decent medical care, and the freedom to speak their mind and worship the religion of their choice. They didn't care if they lived under a communist or a democratic government, as long as they were treated decently and provided with the necessities they needed.

But to the United States, that did not matter. If they supported communism, any type of communism, they supported the enemy. Believing that any means to end the Cold War were justified, the U.S. sent billions of dollars in weapons, supplies, and money to the Salvadoran military, and gladly offered training and education to their soldiers.

While Father Romero sympathized with the peasants and their plight and tried to help them in small ways, it was widely known that he was a follower and not a leader. Unwilling to take any action that might go against the government, Romero openly denounced the campesinos who wanted to fight for their rights. Consistently preaching a theme of non-violence, the priest geared his sermons to both the peasants and the soldiers.

It was Father Romero's belief that the best way to unite all members of a nation was by spreading the word of God, and he realized that modern technology could go a long was in helping him do this. Many of the campesinos did not attend church because they felt unwelcome by their 'higher class' peers, and of course very few of the soldiers attended either.

But Romero had thought of a way to bring his message to all the people of El Salvador.

Knowing that the peasants were far too poor to own television sets, Romero was aware that most did have radios. The priest had not forgotten the success Adolph Hitler had in using this device during WWII, and he was able to convince five radio stations to broadcast his Sunday sermons and get his message out to all the country.

Over the years, Romero gained a large following in both his parishes and his radio broadcasts. But little by little, his superiors began delegating more and more administrative duties to him, drastically cutting into his ministry. Although he still served as pastor of the Cathedral Parish of Santo Domingo, and was Chaplain of the Church of San Francisco, he was also appointed executive secretary of the Episcopal Council of Central America and Panama, and selected as editor of the Archdiocesan newspaper Orientacion.

In 1970 he was made Auxiliary Bishop, and delegated to assist Archbishop Luis Chavez of the Archdiocese of San Salvador. Archbishop Chavez was the complete opposite of Romero. Where Oscar was conservative, Chavez was a promoter of liberation theology, a movement that interpreted the words of Jesus as a liberation from unjust economic, political and social conditions. The peasants of San Salvador had embraced liberation theology, but the Catholic Church had not. The stand of the Roman Catholic Church was still non-violence and compliance.

Father Romero took the same stand as the church, and as a result, he was never content or relaxed working with the Archbishop. He obeyed whatever Chavez ordered him to do, but he was never comfortable doing it. In 1974, when Romero was appointed Bishop of Santiago de Maria, it was with great relief that he left the Archdiocese.

But if Father Romero hoped to go back to a simple and peaceful ministry, he was sadly mistaken. The resistance to political and economic oppression was growing all over the country of El Salvador. The campesinos were tired of watching their children die because they had no access to simple antibiotics and seeing their elderly starve to death because they had no money for food. Many of the peasants openly preached that a revolution was at hand and they needed to take up arms to destroy the hated and despised government. Others wanted to bring about change through the preaching of the Gospel. Regardless of which side you gravitated to, there was little doubt that things were heating up in the country.

Conditions had continued to deteriorate for the El Salvadoran peasants, and their treatment by the country's military remained brutal and sadistic. The government of El Salvador cared not in the least for the plight of their fellow countrymen, and they tolerated no complaints from them. Having nowhere else to turn, the peasants looked to the Catholic Church for a solution to their problems. With their displeasure mounting, the campesinos began forming small Christian communities that drew thousands of followers.

The Salvadoran government was not happy with these communities, which they deemed to be 'subversive and Marxist activities', and they ordered the military to 'take care of' anyone who appeared to be opposing the government, including priests, nuns, teachers, and any type of human rights worker.

In order to accommodate such an enormous task, and ensure that that no 'Marxists insurgents' escaped the net, the military enlisted the aid of 'death squads.'

Comprised of brutal and barbaric men who roamed the countryside killing men, women and children at will, the death squads were the most feared of any military-like group in the country. They were indiscriminate in their choice of victim, and encouraged to kill as many as possible by offers of a bounty for each person they exterminated. This money was paid for by the El Salvador hierarchy, rightwing businessmen, and rich landowners who needed the slave labor of the Salvadoran peasants.

If the death squads did not execute a campesino on sight, they would kidnap them off the street, brutally torture them to reveal anything they knew about peasant insurgents plotting against the government, and then kill them by either strangulation, slitting their throats, or injecting them with poison. Many simply disappeared after that, leaving family and friends to wonder whether they had been murdered or exiled from the country.

The death squads were exceptionally successful at wreaking havoc and terrifying the peasant people, but they failed to quell their growing determination to end their oppression any way they could. The peasants continued to stage peaceful protests, and take to the streets to denounce the injustices being perpetrated against them.

And throughout all of this, Father Romero remained passively neutral, preaching non-violence to both the campesinos, and the military 'death squads'. He continued to appear with government officials at public events, and refused to interfere, or speak out against, the decisions they made regarding the country.

CHAPTER 2

On June 21, 1975 in the peasant town of Tres Calles, a small village in Bishop Romero's diocese, a raid took place that locals would later come to call 'massacre in three streets'. It began when the El Salvadoran National Guard was ordered to raid the village on a tip that several of the peasant farmers were meeting and organizing to form a resistance movement.

The guardsmen were to search each house for concealed weapons, and begin at the home of Jose Alberto Ostorga, the alleged mastermind of the plot. It was believed that it was in Ostorga's house that the meetings were being held.

Inside the small adobe and mud hut, Jose Ostorga and his son Jorge watched as the guardsmen approached. The two men were terrified, and Jorge was crying, begging his father not to open the door. But Jose was afraid to disobey, and telling his son to go and hide, Jose opened the door. The guardsmen rushed in, brandishing rifles and machetes.

Jose Alberto was the first to die, cut down by a rifle shot, but he would not be the last. By the time dawn broke on the morning of June 22nd, five bodies would litter three streets in the tiny village of Tres Calles.

The dead were Jose Alberto Ostorga, Jorge Alberto Ostorga, Jose Alfredo Ostorga, Santos Morals and Francisco Morales. Each had been hacked to pieces by machete blows. The scene was gruesome and terrifying. Body parts had been dismembered and scattered throughout the streets.

While people in the village wailed in grief and terror, the guardsmen departed, leaving a scene of absolute carnage in their wake.

Upon learning of the massacre, Bishop Romero rushed to Tres Calles and was appalled by what had happened there. For the first time, he was seeing close up what the peasants of El Salvador lived with every day, and it affected him deeply. He comforted the families of the murder victims, and held mass for the dead. Preaching to those present, Romero's sermon was loud, forceful and angry. He condemned the unfounded violence, and those who had perpetrated it, calling it 'a grim violation of human rights.'

The reality of what Bishop Romero saw in Tres Calles left him feeling obligated to finally do something. That very day, after saying mass for those who had died, he sat down and wrote a letter of protest to the Salvadoran President, Arturo Armando Molina. The letter was ignored.

He then went to those responsible for the massacre, personally visiting the local Commander of the National Guard. There, Romero vehemently denounced the attack and insisted that those who perpetrated it be brought to justice.

The commander sat quietly and listened to the Bishop's tirade. When he finally finished, the commander stood and pointed his finger directly at Father Romero's face.

"Cassock's (the clerical robes priests wear) are not bulletproof." He said, turning around and dismissing the Bishop.

Father Romero took the comment for what it was; a threat on his life.

After the massacre in Tres Calles, Bishop Romero began to visit the members of his diocese regularly, something he had not done in the past. Riding around the countryside on horseback, the priest listened as the peasants told him of their troubles and their tales of horror. They spoke of working 16 hour days on the huge coffee plantations and not being paid for their labor, or being paid only sporadically.

They told how any requests for the back wages were often met with severe beatings that left them unable to work for weeks.

They told him of children dying from common and readily treatable illnesses, because they were not able to afford basic medical care. Repeatedly, he heard tales of no money, little food, murders, disappearances, and people living in a constant state of fear.

Bishop Romero kept a diary, and he recorded all these encounters in it. He began taking money from his diocese, and from his own pocket, to help whenever he could. Although he had always believed that fighting and violence were never the answer to any problems, his thoughts and ideas on this were beginning to change as he saw firsthand the horrors that the campesinos lived with every day.

He still believed that their problems could be solved by adhering to the words of the gospel, but he was finally beginning to understand that this could only succeed if every man was willing to adhere to them. What good would it do the peasants to adhere, if the Salvadoran hierarchy did not? The turning point for Romero came the day he saved a little girls life by simply providing her with penicillin. That night, he wrote in his diary;

> 'The world of the poor teaches us that liberation will arrive only when the poor are not simply on the receiving end of handouts from the government and churches, but when they themselves are the masters and protagonists of their own struggle for liberation.'

On February 20, 1977, El Salvador held its presidential election, and General Carlos Humberto Romero, (no relation to Oscar), was appointed president. The election was obviously fraudulent, and this fact greatly upset and angered the peasants, but there was little they could do about it.

As if to add insult to injury, three days later, on February 23, 1977, when Archbishop Luis Chavez reached the mandatory age of retirement, Bishop Oscar Romero was appointed Archbishop of El Salvador. Both the peasants, and those clergy who had embraced liberation theology, were unhappy with Romero's advancement. Since no one was aware of his changing views, the new Archbishop was still seen as a highly conservative priest who would not interfere with the government.

If things had been bad for the campesinos before Carlos Romero became president of El Salvador, they were about to become much worse. Eight days after he took office, as crowds gathered in the streets to protest the election fraud, the new president ordered his police to fire upon them, killing dozens.

Abuse such as this was common for the peasants, but now harassment of the clergy began in earnest too. By the beginning of March, three foreign priests had been abducted by members of the El Salvador military, and ejected from the country. A Salvadoran priest was kidnapped by a death squad, beaten to within an inch of his life, and had his battered body thrown through the chancellery doors as a warning to others.

Whatever small amount of respect the Catholic Church may have held with the oligarchy and government, it appeared to end the day General Carlos Romero became president. This, despite the fact that they now believed, with Oscar Romero appointed Archbishop, they had an ally in the Catholic Church.

If the campesinos were unhappy about Romero's appointment to Archbishop, the El Salvador oligarchy and its military were not. They expected Romero's passive nature to go a long way in bringing their subjects back under control, and they were not the only ones who felt this way.

Just like his good friend Rutilio Grande, many others in the priesthood were concerned with Romero's appointment, fearing that he would put a halt to liberation theology, and cancel out any progress those fighting for the peasants had made.

Romero seemed to confirm these fears when, shortly after his appointment, twenty protestors were shot by military police in the Cathedral of San Salvador. Although the new Archbishop denounced the violence, he appeared to take no further action against those responsible.

Those who feared the new Archbishop would remain passive to the plight of the oppressed may have been right. Despite Oscar Romero's changing attitude, he still might have been inclined to keep his church separate from the state. But if so, that all changed with the murder of his much admired friend, Father Rutilio Grande.

The death squads had been sent to assassinate Father Grande for two reasons; the first was because of his preaching, which they felt was inciting the peasants to rebel, and the second was simply a warning to the new Archbishop to desist from preaching the same.

But it was a warning that completely backfired.

On March 12th, when Rutilio Grande and his two companions were brutally killed by one of El Salvador's death squads, Archbishop Oscar Romero experienced a true and complete transformation. He was devastated by the loss of his friend, deeply grieved, sickened, and absolutely furious.

The ravaged bodies of the three murdered men had been carried to a small hut by sugar cane workers who witnessed the ambush. Archbishop Romero traveled to the house as soon as he got word of the assassination, and there he offered a mass for the repose of his good friend and the two innocent peasants who had died with him.

The campesinos who crowded around were inconsolable, and each spoke to Romero of the good deeds that Father Grande had done for them. The new Archbishop knew that they were grieving for their lost champion, but he was deeply inspired to see that their faith remained as strong as ever. All of them proclaimed that they knew Jesus would send them a new savior to fight for them.

When Oscar Romero returned home that night, he thought a lot about what the peasants had said. Writing in his diary, he made it clear that he believed God was calling him to become the new redeemer for the oppressed people of El Salvador.

On March 14th, two days after Father Grande's death, the Archbishop conducted his funeral and celebrated mass at the San Salvador Cathedral. One hundred other priests officiated alongside him, and the crowd was so massive that it spilled from the church to the plaza outside. For the first time since he was appointed Archbishop, Romero gave the peasants of his country a glimmer of hope.

Calling Father Grande and his two companions 'co-workers in Christian liberation', he went on to send a message directly to the government and military of El Salvador.

"The government should not consider a priest, who takes a stand for social justice, to be a politician or a subversive element when he is fulfilling his mission in the politics of the common good!" Romero cried, and then, much to the surprise of his fellow priests, he publicly stated that if any members of the assassination team were Catholic, he was now excommunicating them from the church.

Even though Romero was pleased that the announcement brought cheers from the campesinos, he knew that it would not sit well with the oligarchy of the country. And he didn't care.

###

Throughout the following week, Archbishop Romero twice contacted president general Carlos Romero to demand that the government investigate the murders of Father Grande and his two companions. President Romero never came right out and refused, but it was obvious that his words of sympathy were meant to pacify the Archbishop and nothing more. When Romero continued to persist, he was answered by having two priests from Father Grande's parish expelled from the country.

But the Archbishop refused to be intimidated. The president general's reluctance to investigate the murders infuriated Oscar Romero and finally convinced him that the peasants had been right. The government was in the pocket of the El Salvadoran aristocracy, who were determined to keep the campesinos oppressed for little more than personal gain.

Realizing for the first time that his unwillingness to speak out about the government's treatment of the peasant population had been a silent approval of it, the Archbishop found himself deeply ashamed. He prayed for guidance, and studied his scriptures, finally coming to the conclusion that the situation was not a conflict between the church and state, but a conflict between the government and its people.

In other words, the church was not entering the conflict, but was drawn into it simply because they were backing the people rather than the government. And, for the first time, he also came to realize that the church's teachings of non-violence were not so cut and dried.

Finally, Oscar Romero came to understand that although the church wanted peace, this was not possible without justice. And if there was no way to get justice, no peaceful road to take, the only remaining choice was to rebel.

Firmly believing now that it was his duty to speak for and aid those who had no one else to do it for them, Archbishop Romero decided to take a stand. He advised the Salvadoran government that he would no longer allow any representative of the Archdiocese to appear with a government official at public events. And he went a step further by announcing that he was cancelling all masses throughout the country for the following Sunday, with the exception of one. He would hold a mass on the steps of the San Salvador Cathedral, and all Catholics were invited to attend.

The single mass was meant to be a form of protest, and Romero hoped the peasants of El Salvador would come out in full force. He was well pleased to see that they did not disappoint him. More than 100,000 people showed up, cramming inside the cathedral, and mobbing the plaza outside. When the Archbishop made the statement that 'to know God is to do justice', the crowd erupted in a deafening cheer.

The El Salvadoran government was shocked by this brazen act from a man they believed would be an asset to them, and they were highly critical of it. They were joined in their feelings by several priests from the Catholic Church too, but Romero did not care.

Although the mass had been a great success in bandying the peasant population together, it left the Salvadoran government and its military wondering if appointing Oscar Romero Archbishop was the biggest mistake they ever made.

CHAPTER 3

Much to the surprise of the entire country, Archbishop Romero became a stronger champion for the rights of the El Salvador peasants than anyone who had come before him. But he knew he would not have an easy fight. The church was being persecuted and accused of instigating 'rioters', and priests and nuns were being abused and harassed.

The first thing Romero did after his transformation was to establish an Archdiocesan commission to document human rights abuses in his country, and in retaliation, the Salvadoran military executed another priest. Father Alfonso Navarro was shot to death outside the city of San Salvador on May 11, 1977. Shortly thereafter, another priest was arrested and charged with organizing a demonstration in which 8 protesters were killed by police. This, despite the fact that at the time of the demonstration the priest, Father Jorge Sarsanedas, was saying mass miles away.

If the government hoped these acts would scare Archbishop Romero into submission, they were completely mistaken. If anything, they spurred the new crusader on to fight even harder.

Romero sat down and wrote a letter to President Jimmy Carter of the United States, appealing to his Christianity, and begging the president to cease sending aid to the Salvadoran military. 'Your money is simply used to kill my people,' he wrote. Although his pleas went unnoticed, that did not slow him down.

Archbishop Romero became a virtual writing machine in the following days and weeks. He wrote to the United Nations, to the leaders of other countries, and to his fellow bishops, asking all for their help and support in ending the oppression of his people. His letters went unanswered, and only one fellow bishop agreed to stand with him.

But Romero refused to be dismayed. If he had to stand alone, then so be it. No matter how many times he was shot down, he would continue to work towards an end to the social injustices being perpetrated against his fellow countrymen.

Although the Salvadoran government and its military, had no intention of cowering down to the likes of Oscar Romero, they were hesitant to do anything to him personally. The man was, after all, an Archbishop. But that did not stop them from sending him a clear message of how unhappy they were.

The death toll among the peasants began to rise, and mutilated bodies were left in plain sight along roadways. On August 4th, in a most dramatic and public way, the Salvadoran army killed another priest, Father Alidio Napoleon Macias.

Only the week before, Father Macias had published an article in the diocesan newspaper listing the assassinations committed by the military working in his parish district. Angry death squad members entered the church where Macias was saying mass and gunned him down as he stood on the pulpit.

In 1979, four priests were assassinated, along with hundreds of union workers, lay ministers, students and peasants. Nearly 3,000 people, most of them campesinos, were being murdered each month, and the fear of a civil war was about to become a reality.

Archbishop Oscar Romero was heartbroken by what was happening to his people, and he continued to call for an end to the destruction and devastation. He used his radio broadcasts each week to report on the conditions in El Salvador - the abuses being performed against innocent people, the disappearances of peasants, clergymen, and religious workers, and the death tolls. And every week he would rally his countrymen to keep their faith and not lose hope. He reminded them that good would come from evil, and that they and their families would not die in vain.

Romero's life had been threatened numerous times, and he knew he was unpopular with the hierarchy of the country. But if he was afraid, he never showed it. While speaking to a reporter one day, the Archbishop told him, "You can tell the people that if they succeed in killing me, that I forgive and bless those who do it. Hopefully they will realize they are wasting their time. A bishop will die, but the church of God, which is the people, will never perish."

Things in El Salvador had changed, and President Romero was losing control. He had ordered an increase in the violence against his subjects, but the peasants were no longer the meek and timid people he had once terrorized into submission. They were still afraid, and still dying in untold numbers, but they were not backing down. The President General's country was about to erupt into a full-blown civil war, and he put the blame for it squarely on Archbishop Romero and those who fought with him.

The El Salvador president was unwilling to compromise in any way where the hated campesinos were concerned, and he was prepared to let a war erupt in his country before he would lower himself to negotiate with peasants. But others in the government and the military were not.

In the hopes of avoiding a civil war, a civil-military group had formed calling themselves the Revolutionary Government Junta, or JRG. Comprised of three civilians and two army Colonels, Adolfo Majano and Jaime Gutierrez, the group's members held different motives for wanting to prevent a civil war.

Colonel Majano was a true reformist, who wanted Romero out of power to try and bring peace to his country, while Colonel Gutierrez was fiercely anti-communist and wanted Romero out because he feared that if a war broke out, Romero would not be able to stop the communist peasants from gaining power.

On October 15, 1979, in a coup led by Majano and Gutierrez, the JRG ousted President General Carlos Romero and seized power of El Salvador. The new Junta immediately put into effect some land reforms, and announced that they intended to turn the economic situation around too, by nationalizing the coffee and sugar industries, and bringing better wages to its workers.

But the last thing the oligarchy of El Salvador wanted was a redistribution of wealth and property. They resisted the policies of JRG, and in so doing made it impossible for the new Junta government to implement any of their ideas.

Soon, problems arose within the JRG between the two army colonels and the three civilians, and the civilians quickly resigned. They were easily replaced, but trouble still brewed.

Gutierrez wanted Majano out, and to help achieve this he enlisted the aid of Defense

Minister Colonel Guillermo Garcia. Garcia undermined the new government by excluding Majano's supporters and key players from advancements or important positions, oftentimes transferring them to different areas.

Although the new government Junta publicly denounced the wanton murder of the campesinos, the death toll continued to rise. The majority of these killings were committed by the National Guard, the Police, and newly formed death squads who were, to some extent, secretly sanctioned by Colonel Gutierrez and Defense Minister Colonel Garcia. Colonel Majano was seen as a traitor of the worst kind, someone who had betrayed not only his army, but his country as well.

When, in early 1980, another member of the new Junta resigned, Jose Napoleon Duarte entered the picture. Duarte had served as mayor of San Salvador from 1964 to 1970, and became very popular with the people. In 1972, when he ran for president and was defeated by Arturo Molina, there was widespread speculation that Molino had fixed the election. In retaliation, Duarte's supporters attempted a failed coup to overthrow the new president and Duarte was quickly arrested. Tried for high treason and condemned to death, it was only because of international pressure that Duarte's life was saved. He was exiled from the country, and went to live in Venezuela.

He had only recently returned to El Salvador, and on March 3, 1980, he joined the Junta and became foreign minister of El Salvador. By the end of the year his position would be elevated to head of state, and head of the Junta.

But Duarte's appointment to foreign minister was too late to stop a revolution. The insurrection was already underway, despite the fact that the Junta had come to power to prevent an uprising, El Salvador was thrust into the throes of civil war.

From that point on, conditions for members of the Roman Catholic Church went downhill quickly. The harassment and abuse implemented against the clergy, nuns, missionaries and parishioners was shameful. These people, typically regarded as holy and accustomed to being held in respect, were now treated lower than snakes.

On March 23, 1980, Archbishop Romero held his regular Sunday mass over the radio, reporting on the violence that had occurred that week, and the number of casualties and disappearances that befell his fellow countrymen, and then Archbishop Romero did something he had never done before.

Speaking from the heart, he directed his words to the military soldiers who were carrying out the order's to massacre the innocent.

> "Bothers, you are from the same people," he cried, "You kill your fellow peasants. No soldier is obliged to obey an order that is contrary to the will of God. In the name of God, in the name of this suffering people, I ask you, I implore you, I command you, in the name of God; stop the repression!"

The military leaders were stunned. The '14 families' were shocked. And those opposed to freeing the peasants from their oppression were furious. Just who did the Archbishop think he was to give them orders? To command them to do anything? This time, Oscar Romero had gone too far.

Only two days before Archbishop Romero directed his sermon to the El Salvadoran military, he had been summoned to the home of his friend Jorge Pinto. Pinto's mother had passed away, and Romero had readily agreed to say the requiem mass at her funeral.

The funeral took place on March 24, 1980 in a small chapel inside the hospital of La Divina Providencia, in the north of San Salvador. If Romero gave any thought to the sermon he had given just the day before, which had so infuriated the Salvadoran hierarchy, he made no mention of it.

The draped coffin rested before the pulpit on which Romero stood to say mass and offer comfort to the woman's grieving family. Near the end of the funeral, the Archbishop gave communion to the gathering crowd, the most sacred part of the ceremony, and began to speak his closing remarks.

At that point, the doors of the chapel opened and two men, dressed in suits, one carrying a camera, entered the church. Jorge Pinto was the publisher of the newspaper El Independiente, and those who turned to look assumed the men were members of the press.

The two men began walking up the center aisle as the Archbishop continued with the mass, never missing a beat with his words. When they were just before the pulpit, one of them raised the camera and took a picture, blinding the priest momentarily with the flash. Simultaneously, a shot rang out, sending a .22 caliber bullet directly into the Archbishops chest. Instantly, a huge scarlet stain began to spread across the priest's cassock. His eyes widened in surprise for a moment, and then, almost in slow motion, he began to crumple to the floor.

A scream rang out from the pews, and in a rush, horrified mourners began to clamber towards the pulpit. Amidst the shock and ensuring pandemonium, the two killers slipped unnoticed out of the chapel.

Archbishop Oscar Romero, the man who had vowed to stay neutral, and then rose to become one of the greatest champions the Salvadoran people ever had, lay dead on the pulpit of the little church.

CHAPTER 4

The assassination of Archbishop Oscar Romero sent shock waves throughout El Salvador and many parts of the world. The campesinos were devastated and grief stricken, having lost the most vocal supporter they had yet had. But if the military regime had hoped the death of Romero would bring a halt to the war, they were woefully mistaken.

Instead, it had the opposite effect. The assassination of their beloved savior catapulted the peasants to fight harder, making them more determined than ever to ensure that Romero had not died in vain. They retaliated quickly, and violently.

Around 5:00 am, less than twelve hours after the Archbishop's assassination, 12 bombs exploded around the city of San Salvador, mainly in upper-class neighborhoods, and near office and governmental businesses.

Immediately, twenty-one American officials were evacuated and flown to Guatemala, and the Salvadoran military and security forces were put on high alert. The city remained tense all day, and nearly deserted.

The next day, March 26th, 10,000 people accompanied the coffin carrying Oscar Romero on a 12 block march around the city of San Salvador. The Archbishop was carried from the Basilica to the Cathedral steps, and although security forces were in place, they did not antagonize the procession. They did, however, keep many people from joining it, on the grounds of 'possible danger.'

The only sound from the mourners was an eruption of applause as the coffin was carried up the Cathedral steps. At the same time, the United States sent a telegram to the Embassy of San Salvador denouncing the assassination, and urging the Salvadoran government to 'swiftly and effectively bring the Archbishop's assassins to justice.'

On March 30, Oscar Romero's funeral was held at the Cathedral in San Salvador with an astonishing 50,000 people or more attending. Peasants travelled for days, and from all over the country, to pay their final respects to the man who had fought so hard for them. Pope John Paul II sent a delegate in his place, Cardinal Corripio Ahumada, to eulogize the murdered Archbishop.

Viewing the massive crowd as a 'protest', the Salvadoran oligarchy ordered the military to position snipers on rooftops of nearby buildings, allegedly to keep order and control.

In the square outside the cathedral, where 45,000 mourners waved palm fronds and sang hymns, a bomb suddenly exploded in the crowd. Immediately, chaos erupted as another bomb went off, incinerating a parked car and showing the street with shrapnel. People began screaming and running, trying to get out of the fenced in square. Almost simultaneously, two more bombs exploded and three more vehicles were engulfed in flames.

With at least four fires burning out of control, the massive crowd pushed and shoved each other, trying to flee and knocking people to the ground as they did so. Seeing the pandemonium below, the snipers on the rooftops soon opened fire, killing many who had come to mourn. The entire scene was one of bedlam and chaos. Inside the cathedral, the funeral mass was abandoned, and the body of Archbishop Romero was hastily buried in a crypt beneath the sanctuary.

When everything was said and done, more than 40 innocent people had been killed at the Archbishops funeral, and thousands more seriously injured. Some had been felled by snipers bullets, but others had been trampled to death as those gathered stormed the exits. It appeared that even in death, the Salvadoran military would not let Oscar Romero rest.

Although the world reacted with shock to the Archbishop's assassination, no real investigation was ever done into his murder, and no one ever came forward to take credit for it. But eight months after the Archbishop's assassination, on November 18, 1980, an unidentified source told officials from the American Embassy in San Salvador that Major Roberto D'Aubuisson was the mastermind behind the attack.

Well known and extremely feared, D'Aubuisson had been born in Santa Tecla, El Salvador on August 23, 1944, and graduated from the military academy in 1963 at the age of 19. In 1972, he traveled to Panama to be educated at the United States School of the Americas.

Created and run by the United States Department of Defense, the School of the Americas provided military training for government officials of Latin American countries, and was established to aid in the Cold War against communism. Over the years, the school would educate many Latin American Dictators, including Manuel Noriega.

After completing his education at the School of the Americas, where he was taught the use of torture during interrogation, D'Aubuisson joined the Salvadoran Army military intelligence, rising to the rank of major. Beginning in 1978, D'Aubuisson became a leader of the brutal death squads that indiscriminately slaughtered thousands of campesinos around the country.

Between his training at the School of the Americas and his work in military intelligence, D'Aubuisson became adept at using torture during interrogations. He was a brutal and terrifying man who was given the nickname 'blowtorch Bob' because of his frequent use of a blowtorch during interrogations.

According to the unidentified source who contacted the U.S. Embassy, D'Aubuisson had called a meeting only two days before Romero was murdered to plan the Archbishop's assassination. To see which one of them would have the honor of killing the hated Archbishop, the men gathered at the meeting had drawn straws. The winner, again according to the source, had been an ex-National Guardsmen, and the source himself had provided the ammunition for the weapon.

The U.S. Embassy certainly knew that D'Aubuisson had reason to want Oscar Romero dead, and was more than capable of committing the crime. Only six weeks after the assassination, he, along with several soldiers and some civilians, were all arrested on an isolated farm outside San Salvador. The charge was plotting to overthrow the El Salvador Junta government and assassinate Colonel Majano, a fact that was confirmed by the unidentified source.

According to him, Majano needed to die before December 20th to 'demonstrate a new resolve before the Reagan administration took office in the United States'. Majano, however, would not die. Instead, he would be ousted from the Junta Government and sent into exile on December 7, 1980.

Inside the farmhouse, the raiders found a huge cache of weapons and documents identifying D'Aubuisson and the others as leaders of the military death squads.

Rather than try D'Aubuisson, who was held in great esteem by many, the Junta exiled him to Guatemala, much to the infuriation of those who supported him. In retaliation, his supporters increased their terroristic threats and actions, waging a new war of continuous pressure and fear on the hierarchy of the country. The campaign worked, and within only a short time, D'Aubuisson was allowed to come back to El Salvador.

Once he returned, the alleged assassin of Archbishop Romero seemed to be the most feared man in the country. He spent a tremendous amount of time broadcasting on television, denouncing the Junta government and all of his known enemies. He mentioned names and places, and many of those D'Aubuisson condemned turned up dead right after his television appearances.

Roberto D'Aubuisson would continue to speak out against the JRG, and wreak havoc around the country of El Salvador. And no one would do anything to stop him.

Throughout all this time, the United States Government continued to send aid to El Salvador, thus helping to enable them to continue killing their own people on a massive scale.

Although the majority of the American public criticized President Jimmy Carter for helping the Latin American country, Carter chose to ignore them. But in December of 1980, eight months after the assassination of Archbishop Romero, an event would occur that would force President Carter to re-evaluate his position.

In early 1980, as the civil war in El Salvador progressed, Archbishop Romero made an appeal to all Catholic clergy for help in aiding and ministering the ravaged people of his country. Hundreds responded to his plea, including many Americans, several of whom came from the neighboring country of Nicaragua where they had been performing the same work.

Four of those answering the Archbishops call were; 42-year-old Dorothy Kazel, 49-year-old Maura Clarke, 40-year-old Ita Ford, and 27-year-old Jean Donovan.

Dorothy Kazel, an Ursuline nun from Cleveland Ohio, had become a member of the Cleveland Latin American Mission team in 1974, and was sent to El Salvador where she taught the peasants how to read and write, and showed the young mothers how to care for their children. After the war broke out, when friends and family suggested Dorothy return home where it was safe, Dorothy told them, 'I could not leave Salvador, especially now – I am committed to the persecuted church here.'

Maura Clarke, a nun with the Maryknoll Sisters in New York, had begun her missionary work in 1959 in Nicaragua where she became known as 'the angel of our land'. When Archbishop Romero sent out his appeal, Maura left Nicaragua and travelled to El Salvador, where she helped the refugees of the increasingly violent war. She wrote home that her work was 'real concern for the victims of injustice in today's world – for the sufferings of the poor and marginated, the non-persons of our human family.'

Ita Ford was also a nun of the Maryknoll Sisters and had arrived in El Salvador the day of Oscar Romero's funeral. There she worked with another Maryknoll sister, Carla Piette, helping the poor by providing food, shelter and transportation to them. In August, the two nuns were caught in a flash flood while driving, and Sister Carla, in a heroic action, pushed Ita from the car. The brave nun saved Ita Ford's life that day, but she herself was not so fortunate. Carla Piette couldn't get out of the car and she perished in the flood, devastating Ita Ford.

It was after Sister Carla's death the Ita would be joined by her fellow Maryknoll sister Maura Clarke, who was already in El Salvador, and the two would continue to work together to aid and minister to the county's war-torn poor.

Jean Donovan was the youngest of the four women, an attractive, generous and compassionate girl who had one day quit her executive accounting job, gave all her belongings away, and joined the Maryknoll lay mission. She had been sent to El Salvador in 1977, and had worked closely with Oscar Romero. The two became good friends, and each Sunday Jean would bring the Archbishop a plate of home baked cookies after his mass. Romero's assassination devastated the young missionary, and she was at his funeral when chaos broke out and 40 innocent peasants were killed.

Unlike Maura, Ita and Dorothy, who were all nuns, Jean was only a lay missionary, working in a very dangerous environment. She wrote home of her fears, telling friends that she witnessed people being killed on a daily basis. She admitted the terror she felt when three people from her area were kidnapped, tortured and hacked to death with machetes, and the guilt and pain she experienced only days later when two of her best friends were murdered after walking her home.

Jean's friends and family, appalled by what she was living with, urged her to leave the country and return home. Jean seriously thought about doing that, and she wrote to a friend that she would if it weren't for the children. She worried about who would care for them, writing; 'Whose heart could be so staunch as to favor the reasonable thing, in a sea of tears and loneliness? Not mine, dear friend, not mine.'

The four women would continue to give of their time and energy to help those less fortunate – men, women and children they had never even met. They were all kind, compassionate, god-fearing women. And each of them were American.

###

On the afternoon of December 2, 1980, Jean Donovan and Dorothy Kazel drove to the Comolopa International Airport in San Salvador to pick up two Maryknoll missionary sisters who had been attending a conference in Nicaragua. Unbeknownst to them, Jean and Dorothy were under surveillance from the El Salvadoran National Guard.

When the national guardsmen saw the women leaving the airport, they phoned their commander and asked what they should do. Their commander ordered them to change into plain clothes, and continue surveillance on the airport.

Later that evening, Jean and Dorothy returned to the airport to pick up Maura Clarke and Ita Ford, who had attended the same conference in Nicaragua. This time, when the four women left the airport driving a white van, the five national guardsmen, now out of uniform, followed them.

Just outside of San Salvador, the guardsmen stopped the van and forced their way inside. Driving them to an isolated spot in a rural setting, the five men beat the women brutally, tortured them, raped them, and then murdered them.

Peasants working in the fields noticed the white van pass by, and later heard machine gun fire followed by single shots from a rifle. Within only minutes of hearing the gunfire, the peasants saw the white van returning, traveling at a high rate of speed with the lights on and the radio blaring.

Early the next morning, the peasants who had witnessed the van's coming and going went to investigate. There, they found a gruesome and grisly sight. The bodies of the four churchwomen, lying in a tangled jumble, bruised, battered and shot to death.

Immediately the peasants went to summon help, and were shocked when local authorities ordered them to bury the bodies in a nearby field. The campesinos did as they were told, praying as they completed their task, and marking the site with a crude cross made from two broken branches. They had been ordered not to speak of what they had witnessed, but later that same day four of the men would tell their parish priest what had occurred.

The priest was shocked by the disclosure and immediately informed his bishop. He, in turn, immediately informed Robert White, the U.S. Ambassador to El Salvador. The next day, December 4, 1980, in front of fifteen reporters, several missionaries, and Ambassador White, the shallow grave containing the battered bodies of Maura Clarke, Dorothy Kazel, Ita Ford and Jean Donovan was exhumed.

Later that same day the white van that the women had driven was found abandoned and burned close to the San Salvador airport.

On December 5th a mass was held for the murdered women, presided over by Bishop Arturo Rivera Dumas, and the next day the bodies of Jean Donovan and Dorothy Kazel were flown back to the United States for burial. Maura Clarke and Ita Ford would be buried in El Salvador, keeping to the tradition of the Maryknoll Missionaries.

The murders of the four women were brutal, sadistic, and tragic, but no more so than thousands of other women, and even children, who had died horrible deaths in the country of El Salvador. But these four deaths were different. While the others who had died were poor Salvadoran peasants, Ita Ford, Maura Clarke, Dorothy Kazel, and Jean Donovan were American citizens.

And it would be their deaths that finally made people stand up and take notice of what was happening in the Latin American country of El Salvador.

###

News of the murders of the four American women sent shock waves throughout the world, and especially in the United States. Pressure and protesting from the American public finally led President Jimmy Carter to cut off aid to the Latin American country. But that was not enough. America wanted justice for the slain women, and they hounded Carter, demanding that he order El Salvador to conduct an investigation into the deaths.

The Salvadoran government assured the United States that it would, and within days they reported back that the women were the victims of an attempted robbery. It was a ridiculous assessment, and no one believed it, but President Carter, who was under intense pressure from members of congress who supported the Salvadoran war, chose to accept it. The report was enough to allow him to reinstate aid to the war-torn country.

The families of the four women were outraged, and demanded that the U.S. find out what had actually happened to them. But their pleas went unheeded, and it soon became apparent that the U.S. was treating the matter as a closed case.

Ita Ford's brother Bill had no intention of letting his government sweep his sister's murder under a rug. He wanted answers, and he wanted justice. Loud and vocal, he rallied support from family members and the public, and took his case before congress. With the growing pressure to do something, the U.S. began a new investigation into the four murders.

The Salvadoran government, feeling the heat from their biggest supporter, finally arrested five National guardsmen in May of 1981. The men were quickly tried, convicted and sentenced to 30 years in prison, and both the U.S. and Salvadoran governments considered that to be the end of the matter.

Thousands of people dedicated their lives to helping the oppressed in El Salvador. They strived to provide an environment of decency, respect, and equality to every man, woman and child living in the country. And the only thing they asked for in return was that the campesinos basic human rights be upheld and preserved. Priests, nuns, missionaries, lay ministers, teachers, human rights activists, and countless others gave up everything they owned, including their very lives, to try and help their fellow man, and each gained little recognition for their selfless acts.

All of them were aware of the consequences they faced, and the danger they lived with every day, yet they stayed anyway, doing what they thought was right. For those who came from America, they had the added burden of knowing that they were fighting not only the Salvadoran government, but their own government as well. It was a bitter pill to swallow, and a realization they found hard to understand.

One day, Ita Ford had read a passage from a priest's sermon that she never forgot. The passage held great meaning to her, because never before had she come across words that so completely explained the feelings of those who risked their lives to save others. On the day before her death, Ita quoted the passage to those parishioners gathered at mass.

> "Christ invites us not to fear persecution because, believe me brothers and sisters, the one who is committed to the poor must run the same fate as the poor, and in El Salvador we know what the fate of the poor signifies; to disappear, to be tortured, to be held captive and to be found dead."

Ironically, Ita Ford was quoting Archbishop Oscar Romero, who had spoken these exact words during one of his last sermons. For both the Archbishop and Ita Ford, along with countless others, the words were irrefutably prophetic.

EPILOGUE

The Salvadoran civil war raged for a total of 12 years and claimed more than 75,000 lives, a casualty total that many people believe to be extremely conservative. The United States continued to aid the Salvadoran military throughout the entire war, and even beyond, contributing billions of dollars in an effort to destroy communism.

Since the civil war's end, things have improved greatly for the campesinos of El Salvador. Their corrupt and brutal leaders have been removed, and a new civilian police force has been created. Land has been transferred back to peasants and refugees, and significant progress has been made in other areas as well. But the country still has its fair share of problems.

There remains a socio-economic class distinction among its residents, and a large percentage of the population is still struggling to survive on pitifully low wages. Crime is rampant in the cities, and health care is still not widely available to the majority of the population. Even today, diarrhea is one of the top three leading causes of illness-related deaths in the country. But as bad as it might be, the residents of El Salvador know it could be worse.

Robert D'Aubuisson, the alleged mastermind of Archbishop Oscar Romero's assassination went on to form the right-wing political party ARENA, (National Republican Alliance), and in 1982 his party won a majority of the legislative seats. Having the majority vote, his party was instrumental in getting Alvaro Magana elected as president of El Salvador and having the JRG dissolved. Jose Napoleon

Duarte was head of the Junta at the time, and relinquished his power over to Magana willingly.

But Duarte had a purpose in doing this. He planned to work on his own party, the Christian Democratic Party, and seize back control of the country two years hence. In 1984 he succeeded in doing this when he won the presidential election against Roberto D'Aubuisson.

After the Salvadoran civil war ended in 1992, several secret memos regarding Archbishop Romero's assassination became declassified, and their content was astonishing. Each identified Roberto D'Aubuisson as being the mastermind of the plot. One telegram, dated February 25, 1981 and sent to Washington D.C. not only names D'Aubuisson as being involved, but also members of the Junta government. Specifically Colonel Gutierrez and Defense Minister Colonel Garcia.

According to the telegram, in order to give the appearance of legality, the operation was entrusted to the National Police, who were also assigned the task of conducting a mock investigation into the murder.

Another memo, dated 12/21/81 is deemed a follow up to the November interview conducted with the unidentified source who approached the U.S. Embassy in El Salvador and named D'Aubuisson as the mastermind to Romero's assassination. In this correspondence, the source revealed the name of the actual triggerman as 27-year-old Walter Antonio Alvarez. It goes on to reveal that six months after the assassination, Walter Alvarez himself was murdered. The alleged killer of Archbishop Romero was apparently dragged away from a football game, shot several times, and had his bullet riddled body left on the side of the road.

After the war, both the United Nations and the United States each confirmed that D'Aubuisson "gave the order to assassinate Archbishop Oscar Romero," and ex-U.S. ambassador Robert White publicly stated that; "there was sufficient evidence to convict D'Aubuisson of the assassination."

One has to wonder why, if all this evidence was known within months of the Archbishop's death, no one was ever charged with his murder? Why was the assassination covered up, not only by the Salvadoran government, but by the U.S. government as well?

Those are questions that remain unanswered, and by the time the declassified information came to light, it was impossible to charge Roberto D'Aubuisson with any crime. He was already dead, having died in 1992 at the age of 47, from esophageal cancer.

Bill Ford, the brother of Ita Ford, had fought long and hard to find out what had happened to his sister, and who was responsible for the deaths of her, Maura Clarke, Dorothy Kazel, and Jean Donovan. After 25 years, he finally found some answers.

Again, through declassified information, it was discovered that besides the five National Guardsmen who actually abducted, raped, and carried out the murders, five others were involved with the crime. General Oscar Edgardo

Casanova Vejar, who was commander of the National Guard unit that carried out the attack, Major Lizandro Zepeda Velasco who planned it, and Luis Antonio Colindres Aleman, who gave the actual order to kill the four women. Also involved as accessories before and after the fact were Colonel Carlos Eugenio Vedis Casanova and General Jose Guillermo Garcia.

All five of these men were trained by the United States in their School of the Americas, and even more shocking, two of them, Vedis Casanova and Jose Garcia, were rewarded for their actions by being provided with permanent residency in the United States.

Ex-ambassador Robert White would later declare that he found it hard to believe the United States government didn't know these men were behind the attacks, since he knew almost immediately. He also observed that allowing them 'to be let off not only with their reputations intact, but with the right of residency in the United States does not serve the ends of justice.'

Indeed it doesn't. By the mid 1990's, Garcia and Vedis Casanova were both living in the state of Florida, in relative comfort. If they ever thought about their roles in the senseless and brutal murders of the four churchwomen, it is unlikely they ever worried about it. The Salvadoran government had granted amnesty to all human rights abusers after the war, so they were in no danger of repercussions for their crimes.

But they were unaware of the drive and determination of Bill Ford. Using the evidence they had found, Ford and other family members filed suit against the two Generals now living in Florida. They were allowed to do this under the Torture Victim Protection Act, a law in the United States that gives victims of torture protection anywhere in the world.

In 2000, the two Generals found themselves in a Palm Beach Florida courtroom, facing family members of the four women they were accused of killing, but they were not charged with murder. Instead, the two men were accused of knowing what their troops were doing, and either allowing them to do it, or failing to stop them from doing it.

In November of 2000, the two Salvadorans were found not guilty of the crimes, but their legal troubles were far from over. The families of the four churchwomen immediately appealed, and other people from El Salvador, now living in the U.S. brought more torture charges against them. Eventually, both generals were found guilty of torture crimes unrelated to the four churchwomen, and ordered to pay over 50 million dollars in damages.

The public shouted for the two men to be deported, but each man fought it. The court battles involving Vedis Casanova and Jose Garcia dragged on for years, and both men continued to reside in the United States while they did.

Finally, in 2012 a Florida judge ruled that the two generals could be deported from the U.S, although deportation hearings for each man would still have to be held. Whether Jose

Garcia or Vedis Casanova will ever be ordered out of the United States remains to be seen.

Ita Ford, Maura Clarke, Jean Donovan, and Dorothy Kazel became martyrs of the El Salvador war, and have been honored in their hometowns and churches. Portrayals of their lives, work, and brutal deaths have been made into documentaries, plays and movies, all in an effort to keep their memories alive.

Archbishop Oscar Romero too became a martyr in his church, and to his people. Pope John Paul II gave him the title of Servant of God, and he has been recommended for canonization, a process that is still in the works today. For years, thousands of peasants and Christians walked the route that Romero's body traveled after his assassination, and in 2012 the El Salvador government created a 'tourist route' dedicated to him. He has had statues in his honor erected all over the world, and his tomb is one of the biggest tourist attractions in El Salvador.

Although there were countless tragedies, horrors and brutalities perpetrated against thousands of people in El Salvador, perhaps the biggest tragedy was the assassination of Archbishop Oscar Romero.

Romero was making progress in his attempt to not only bring publicity to the campesinos cause, but also to unite his country. It was, in fact, for these reasons alone that he was murdered. Many place the true beginning of the Salvadoran war as the day of his death, and there is no denying that things became more heated and intense after Romero was assassinated.

How might things have been different for the people of El Salvador, and the entire world, if the Archbishop had been allowed to live and continue his work? Oscar Romero experienced a miraculous transformation. He had not been a champion to the peasants until he got a firsthand look at what was happening to them.

Romero strove to remain neutral and seemed almost to turn a blind eye to the suffering of his fellow people. But if he could turn his heart around to the point that he was willing to die for their cause, who else might he have encouraged to undergo such a marvelous transformation? How might he have changed history if his life were not cut short on March 24, 1980?

It is a question worth wondering about, but one that can never be answered.

BIBLIOGRAPHY

http://www.uscatholic.org/culture/social-justice/2009/02/oscar-romero-bishop-poor

http://thewitness.org/agw/mulligan.050802.html

http://ignatiansolidarity.net/blog/2012/03/12/grande/

www.kellogg.nd.edu/romero/pdfs/Biography.pdf

http://www.microsofttransla-
tor.com/bv.aspx?ref=SERP&br=ro&mkt=en-
US&dl=en&lp=ES_EN&a=http%3a%2f%2fmi-
genteinforma.org%2f%3fp%3d17622

http://www.saint-
ben.derby.sch.uk/?page_id=954

http://www.laprensa-sandi-
ego.org/archieve/february15-02/Brutal.htm

http://news.bbc.co.uk/2/hi/ameri-
cas/1220818.stm

http://archive.catholicherald.co.uk/article/13th-
may-1977/3/jesuit-priest-arrested-in-el-salvador

http://archive.catholicherald.co.uk/article/27th-
may-1977/2/el-salvador-expels-jesuits

http://archive.catholicherald.co.uk/article/7th-
september-1979/10/the-churchs-continuing-
mission-against-government-

http://morallowground.com/2010/12/02/on-this-day-1980-american-nuns-kidnapped-raped-murdered-by-american-trained-salvadoran-death-squad/

http://www.npr.org/templates/story/story.php?storyId=8972597

http://www.washingtonpost.com/wp-dyn/content/article/2007/01/28/AR2007012801353_pf.html

http://www.marxist.com/el-salvador-assasination-of-archbishop-romero.htm

http://www.history.com/this-day-in-history/united-states-calls-situation-in-el-salvador-a-communist-plot

http://anusha.com/killnuns.htm

http://cja.org/article.php?list=type&type=545

http://www.pbs.org/itvs/enemiesofwar/perspectives3.html

http://www.gwu.edu/~nsarchiv/NSAEBB/NSAEBB339/index.htm

http://www.ursulinesisters.org/sister-dorothy-kazel

http://www.historycommons.org/entity.jsp?entity=jose_alberto_chele_medrano_1

http://www.boston.com/news/nation/articles/2012/02/24/ex_el_salvador_defense_minister_can_be_deported/

READY FOR MORE?

We hope you enjoyed reading this series. If you are ready to read similar stories, check out other books in the *Cold Case Crimes* series:

Jeff Davis 8: The True Story Behind the Unsolved Murder That Allegedly Inspired True Detective, Season One (By Fergus Mason)

Jefferson Davis Parish has been described as quaint, and in many ways it certainly is. For anyone from a big city much of the area, especially out among the farms, is like a trip in a time machine. For a sleepy rural community, however, Jefferson Davis is a lot more violent than you'd expect, and these days cheap, potent rocks of cocaine are at the root of a lot of that violence.

Crack addicts are famously willing to do just about anything to subsidize their habit so street prostitution has become a real issue, mostly concentrated in the town's poorer neighborhoods south of the railway track. Prostitution – especially on the street – is a dangerous business, so the sheriff's office weren't too surprised when the first one turned up dead. As the body count climbed people started to take notice, but despite all their efforts the killings continued until eight women were dead.

This book traces one of the most fascinating unsolved crimes in the history of Louisiana. In 2014, many believe it became one of the inspirations for the first season of HBO's "True Detective." But the crimes in this book are much more shocking than anything captured on TV.

Annihilation In Austin: The Servant Girl Annihilator Murders of 1885 (By Tim Huddleston)

Murder. Chaos. Outrage. This was the mode in Texas' capital city, Austin from 1884 to 1885. The city had been haunted by a string of bloody murders. Women were not just killed-- they were dragged alive from their beds, taken outside where they were often tortured and then murdered. Six of the victims, all women, were found dead with sharp objects inserted in their ears.

As horrifying as the murders were, what's more horrifying is that the person who committed these heinous acts of violence was never found. To this day it remains one of the most famous unsolved crimes. It has long been suspected by several noted historians that the real killer may have been none other than Jack the Ripper.

Written with gripping, page turning suspense, this book brings you back in time to Austin, Texas, so you can experience the horror and panic for yourself. Faint at heart turn away!

The Axeman: The Brutal History of the Axeman of New Orleans (By Wallace Edwards)

Between 1918 to 1919 a serial killer ran rampant throughout New Orleans. His weapon of choice? The axe. He didn't spare women. Or children. Or even men. There was only one kind of person who could be sparred from the blade of his axe: the home of a person playing jazz music. At least eight people were brutally murdered. Who could have been responsible for this crime, and how was the Mafia connected? Did a corrupt police department intentionally leave this case unsolved?

Come, if you dare, as Absolute Crime takes you on the hunt for one of the most brutal killers who ever lived.

The Galapagos Murder: The Murder Mystery That Rocked the Equator (By Fergus Mason)

The Galapagos Islands are a scientist's haven. Home to rare creatures, it was made famous by Charles Darwin and is the ideal spot for study, relaxation...and murder?

In September 1929 two settlers arrived on the desolate island of Floreana. They dreamed of escaping it all and were living the dream, until an arrogant Baroness and her lovers arrived. Turning an island paradise into a living hell, the Baroness suddenly disappeared without a trace. To this day, no one is sure what happened to her.

This is the story of love, paradise, betrayal, and murder. It will have you thinking twice before you ever yearn to escape to your own tropical paradise!

Young, Queer, and Dead: A Biography of San Francisco's Most Overlooked Serial Killer, The Doodler (By Reagan Martin)

The Zodiac Killer may have been San Francisco's most notorious serial killer, but another equally cruel killer was also stalking the streets at the same time, and, just like the Zodiac Killer, has never been arrested for his crimes. The difference is, while the Zodiac Killer's murder spree was heavily publicized, this other killer, nicknamed The Doodler, went unreported by the media and is nearly unknown today.

How did this ruthless killer become almost forgotten? Because he didn't target helpless women or children--he targeted gays--and in the 70s many people believed they had it coming; if they would just stop being gay, then all would be well.

In this gripping short book, you will go on the trail for one of the most brutal killers who ever lived. Read about why his victims were disregarded by a homophobic press, and how he was positively identified by three escaped victims...only to walk away free without being arrested.

Getting Away With Murder: 15 Chilling Cold Cases That Will Make You Think Twice About Going Outside (By William Webb)

Despite a decline in the number of murders in the United States since the 1960s, thousands go unsolved each year. As of 2013, the solve rate was at an all time low at only 65 percent of the total committed.

The 15 murders profiled in this book were committed between 1958 and 2014. The oldest of the set involves the bizarre murder of Pearl Eaton, one of the famous Ziegfeld Follies Girls of the 1920s. From the beginning, the crime had no leads or suspects and remains among the coldest of the 15 unsolved crimes. The most recent – the murder of four members of the McStay family found buried in the California desert in November 2013 – is under active investigation.

NEWSLETTER OFFER

Don't forget to sign up for your newsletter to grab your free book:

http://www.absolutecrime.com/newsletter

www.ingramcontent.com/pod-product-compliance
Lightning Source LLC
Chambersburg PA
CBHW051031030426
42336CB00015B/2813